A NOTE TO PARENTS

When your children are ready to "step into reading," giving them the right books—and lots of them—is as crucial as giving them the right food to eat. **Step into Reading Books** present exciting stories and information reinforced with lively, colorful illustrations that make learning to read fun, satisfying, and worthwhile. They are priced so that acquiring an entire library of them is affordable. And they are beginning readers with an important difference— they're written on four levels.

Step 1 Books, with their very large type and extremely simple vocabulary, have been created for the very youngest readers. **Step 2 Books** are both longer and slightly more difficult. **Step 3 Books,** written to mid-second-grade reading levels, are for the child who has acquired even greater reading skills. **Step 4 Books** offer exciting nonfiction for the increasingly proficient reader.

Children develop at different ages. **Step into Reading Books,** with their four levels of reading, are designed to help children become good—and interested—readers *faster*. The grade levels assigned to the four steps—preschool through grade 1 for Step 1, grades 1 through 3 for Step 2, grades 2 and 3 for Step 3, and grades 2 through 4 for Step 4—are intended only as guides. Some children move through all four steps very rapidly; others climb the steps over a period of several years. These books will help your child "step into reading" in style!

For Daniel and David
—M. B.

Photo credits: Duff Armstrong: Lincoln's New State Historic Site and the Illinois Historic Preservation Agency. Stephen Douglas; Abraham Lincoln; Judge Davis: Illinois State Historical Library, Springfield, Illinois.

Library of Congress Cataloging-in-Publication Data
Brenner, Martha.
Abe Lincoln's hat / by Martha Brenner ; illustrated by Donald Cook.
    p.   cm. — (Step into reading.   Step 2 book) ISBN 0-679-84977-7 (pbk.) — ISBN 0-679-94977-1 (lib. bdg.)
1. Lincoln, Abraham, 1809–1865—Juvenile literature.   2. Presidents—United States—Biography—Juvenile
literature.   3. Hats—Juvenile literature.   I. Cook, Donald, ill.   II. Title.   III. Series.
E457.905.B74   1994 973.7'092—dc20 [B]   93-31867

Manufactured in the United States of America   11

Lexile 330

Level 2.9

Abe Lincoln's Hat

by Martha Brenner
illustrated by Donald Cook

A Step 2 Book

Random House 🏠 New York

Abe Lincoln didn't have much money.
But when he became a lawyer,
he wanted to look his best.
He bought a long black coat
and a tall black hat.

Every day Abe wore his hat
to his new job.
People noticed the tall man
in the tall hat.

He was friendly to everyone.

When they needed a lawyer,

they remembered him.

Abe lived in Illinois.

His state was mostly wilderness.

Then more and more settlers came.

They built houses and farms

and new towns.

Sometimes they didn't get along.

They argued over land
and animals and money.
Lawyers like Abe could help people
settle their arguments.
They could help people get
a fair trial in court.

Abe Lincoln was a smart lawyer.

People came to him

with all kinds of problems.

He helped them all.

But he had one problem himself.

He forgot to answer letters.

He forgot where

he put important papers.

A good lawyer cannot forget.

Abe wanted to be a good lawyer,

but he was not a good paper-keeper.

What could he do?

Abe had an idea.

His tall hat!

He could push letters deep inside it.

He could stuff notes
into the leather band.

When he took off his hat,
the papers would remind him
what he had to do.

The idea worked, most of the time.

One day some boys

played a trick on Abe.

They tied a string across the street.

They strung it way up high.

Everyone in town could walk under it.

Everyone except Abe.

When Abe walked down the street,

the string knocked off his hat.

Papers flew everywhere!

He bent over to pick them up.

The boys ran out of hiding.

They jumped all over him.

Abe laughed.

He was not mad at the boys.

He liked a good joke.

But the trick did not stop him

from carrying papers in his hat!

Once a lawyer sent Abe a letter.

Abe stuck it in his hat.

The next day, Abe bought a new hat.

He put away his old one.

Weeks later the lawyer wrote again:

"Why didn't you answer my letter?"

Then Abe remembered.

The letter was still in his old hat!

Many towns in Illinois
had no lawyers and no judges.
So every spring and fall,
a judge and some lawyers traveled
from town to town.
Abe went too.
He packed his hat with papers,
his checkbook, and a handkerchief.

At the head of the parade
of lawyers rode the judge.
No one could miss him.
He weighed over 300 pounds.
Two horses pulled his buggy.

Abe's horse was skinny and slow.

His name was Old Buck.

Abe and Old Buck traveled

lonely country roads.

In the snow.

In the rain.

In the mud.

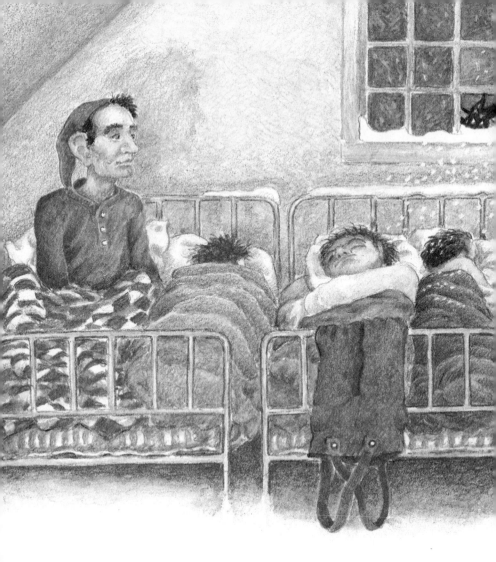

Traveling made Abe very tired.

He dreamed of a soft bed

and a good meal.

But the lawyers had to stay

at poor country inns.

The food was bad.

The rooms were cold.

The beds were crawling with bugs.

The lawyers had to share beds.

Except the judge.

He had his own bed.

Early in the morning

the courthouse bell would ring.

Abe hurried to court.

Pigs lived under one courthouse.

Abe had to talk loudly

over the grunts and squeals.

People came from near and far

to hear Abe.

He made trials easy to understand.

He told jokes and stories.

People said he could make a cat laugh.

Once Abe whispered a joke
to another lawyer.
The lawyer laughed out loud.
"Quiet!" the judge yelled.
"You are fined five dollars."

When the trial was over,

the judge asked to hear the joke.

He laughed as hard as the lawyer.

"That was worth five dollars," he said.

"Forget the fine."

At another trial

two men argued

over who owned a young horse.

Each said he owned

the mother of the colt.

Abe led everyone outside.

He put the two grown horses

on one side of the lawn.

He held the colt on the other side.

Then he set the colt free.

It headed straight to its real mother!

One day Abe got a letter.

It was from Hannah Armstrong.

Years before, Abe had lived

with her family.

Mrs. Armstrong cooked for Abe.

She sewed up the holes in his pants.

Now she begged Abe for help.

Her son Duff was in jail—for murder!

Abe did not stick this letter in his hat.

He wrote back right away:

"Of course I'll help you."

Duff had been in a big fight.

It was very dark.

But a man said

he saw Duff

kill someone.

Duff said he did not do it.

Abe believed Duff.

But how could he prove that

the man was wrong—

or lying?

"How could you see in the dark?"

Abe asked the man.

"The moon was full," the man said.

"It was bright as day."

"Are you sure the moon was full?"

Abe asked again and again.

"Yes," the man repeated.

Then Abe held up

a famous book of facts.

It said there was NO moon

in the sky at the time of the fight!

Now no one believed

the man anymore.

The judge set Duff free!

Abe believed slavery was wrong.

His state had laws against it.

But the laws were not clear.

Many blacks were treated like slaves.

Nance was one of them.

She worked for a storekeeper
who sold her to another man.
This man treated Nance badly.
So she would not work for him.

Abe argued for Nance in court.

Illinois was a free state, he said.

All its people are free,

whatever their color.

The judge decided Abe was right.

From then on, no one could be

bought or sold in Illinois.

Abe had saved Nance.

But half the states in America

still had slaves.

In a few years there would be

new states out west.

Abe did not want slavery to spread

to these states.

Abe tried to get elected
to the U.S. Senate.
If he won, he could make laws
to stop slavery.
He ran against Stephen Douglas.
Douglas argued that each state should
decide for itself if it wanted slaves.
They gave speeches all over Illinois.
Thousands of people heard them.
Abe lost the election but became famous.

In 1860, Abe ran for president.

Stephen Douglas ran too.

This time Abe won.

Abe grew a beard for his new job.

He took his family to Washington.

At every train station, crowds

cheered the new president.

Abe was ready to make

his first speech as president.

He carried a cane, a tall silk hat,

and his speech.

He looked for a place

to put his hat.

Stephen Douglas stepped up.

"If I can't be president,"

he said, "I can at least hold his hat."

Abe Lincoln was a great president.

He freed the slaves.

He worked for fair laws.

He helped unite the nation
after a long war.

But he never changed his ways.

He always kept important papers

in his tall hat!

Judge David Davis

Duff Armstrong

Stephen Douglas

Abraham Lincoln

All the stories in this book are true and
all the people really lived. Here are photos
of some of them. When the photos were taken,
around 1860, the camera was a new invention.